MINIATURE
FLOWERS

MINIATURE

FLWERS

A DESERT SEARCH

Text and photography by
Robert I. Gilbreath

NORTHLAND PRESS  FLAGSTAFF, ARIZONA

FRONTISPIECE
Bean, *Petalostemun evanescens,* 2.17 mm, Prairie Clover

Copyright 1985 by Robert I. Gilbreath
FIRST EDITION
ISBN 0-87358-382-5
Library of Congress Catalog Card Number 85-60940
Composed and Printed in the United States
by Northland Press, Flagstaff, Arizona

ACKNOWLEDGEMENTS

These pictures would not exist at all without the patience, support, and freely given assistance from each of these, to whom I owe full and everlasting gratitude.

Katharine, my wife of more than fifty years, who never flinched or complained when the deserts hit us with the worst of everything they had.

The botanists who spent long hours, even days, delving into their herbariums and reference books to identify the sad and disintegrating specimens that I brought them.

Ira L. Wiggins, Emeritus Professor, Botany
John H. Thomas, Professor, Botany
Department of Biological Sciences,
Stanford University

Alva G. Day, Ph.D., Botany
Frank Almeda, Ph.D., Botany
California Academy of Sciences

Irving McNulty, Professor, Botany
University of Utah

ROBERT I. GILBREATH

MINIATURE

FLOWERS

Spurge, *Euphorbia supina,* 0.82 mm

"In this far-off desert are forms which surprise us by their unaccustomed character."

CLARENCE DUTTON

"This is the sense of the desert hills, that there is room enough and time enough."

MARY AUSTIN

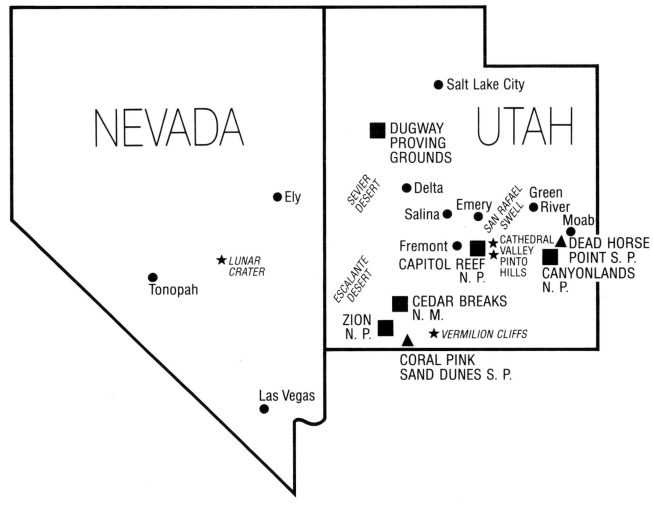

Areas covered in search for miniflowers

INTRODUCTION

"We xerophylophiles do not always agree with one another over the question just where the particular style of beauty which we admire reaches its perfection."

JOSEPH WOOD KRUTCH

One hundred and twelve in the shade and no water for miles. Feet bake inside shoes from the blistering heat of the sand, and skin seems to shrivel under the brazen intensity of the sun and the loss of essential body fluids. There is little respite until after sunset, for there is no hiding from the desert's heat.

The earth is cracked and broken, parched from lack of water. The horizon goes on endlessly, broken occasionally by the brown, jagged peaks of a distant mountain range. The vegetation is sharp and piercing, the wildlife is equipped with thick skin and the agility to scamper from shade to shade. The

Pink, *Spergularia bocconii,* 3.40 mm

intensity and brilliance of the vast, blue sky is rarely pocked with contrasting clouds, and the blazing sun, as it arcs from horizon to horizon, threatens all existence in this desert outback.

It is here—tucked away in a thicket of fearsome-looking spines, in what appear to be tiny balls of cotton, in the shade of a cactus, or partially buried in sand—that the observant hiker will find the tiniest botanical jewels: miniature wildflowers. Measuring no more than four millimeters in diameter, the delicate blooms are exotic treasures. One cannot help but wonder how such fragile life survives under some of the harshest conditions on earth.

Although miniflowers may be found in all parts of the country, they are more abundant in the deserts and semiarid areas of the West and Southwest. They may be found during all seasons except when there is snow or prolonged periods of freezing temperatures. They are almost always found only on ground that has not been disturbed for many years. Some seem to be socially inclined and grow close together in patches, while others exhibit hermitlike qualities and grow singly, far from their nearest neighbor.

Botanists do not know how many species of miniflowers exist; some have estimated that there are as many as 2,000 to 3,000 worldwide. It is conceivable that there may be between 200 and 300 in the North American deserts alone. A botanist can spend a lifetime studying desert plants and never see the flowers of all of them. One must be searching at the exact time of blooming.

As with larger desert flowers, miniflowers do not bloom at regular intervals, that is, annually. They will wait until conditions are precisely to their liking—temperature, moisture, time of year, and perhaps even the proper phase of the moon. When all conditions are prime, they waste no time because the moods of the desert can change abruptly and violently. Even after they start blooming, some disaster—a very hot wind that removes moisture from the ground too rapidly or a sandstorm that scars immature buds and covers small plants—may prevent blooming and seeding for that year.

The ephemeral nature of many of these little flowers and the extremely harsh and remote terrain in which some of them grow account for so relatively little being known about them, even by the most dedicated botanists. The seeds of desert flowers are "timed" to germinate at different intervals to adjust to droughts of varying durations. Poor environmental conditions may exist for years at a time, with one disaster following another. Although a series of disasters and frustrations can last for thirty years or more, when conditions improve and are prime for germination, the plant will bloom and cast its seeds for the next generation.

Miniature flowers are complete in every respect and are equally as complicated as the more common garden and larger wildflowers. These miniscule flowers even have tiny insects that feed upon and pollinize them. Some emit a delicate fragrance, which can be detected if the flowers are growing in a group. These flowers are not dwarfs of larger wildflowers; they are genetically unique.

The size of the blossom determines whether a flower is or is not a true miniflower, and in this respect, there are no established rules among botanists. Each has his or her own criterion. Two fundamental rules of classification follow: First, in its full span, the blossom will measure no more than four millimeters (approximately one-eighth of an inch); and second, when standing or walking over the flower, it cannot be readily seen or recognized. However, sometimes a larger flower (up to 7.5

Plantain, *Plantago purshii,* 3.33 mm

millimeters) will be classified as a miniflower.

There is no certainty that what is seen is a flower until it has been carefully examined with an eight- or ten-power hand glass. Even then, there are times when designation is uncertain; sometimes a very small grain of sand strategically located on a plant can appear to be a flower, particularly if it has color.

The plants on which miniflowers grow are of two general types. The first type includes plants with herbaceous stems of varying firmness and strength. Some of these are annuals, some are perennials. On some plants, the leaves are readily apparent, but on others, the leaves can scarcely be seen at all because they are so small or are on the ground covered with a thin layer of dust and sand. Sometimes the blossom blends so well with the ground that the plant can be found only by the shadow cast by its thin, translucent stem; one then looks for the flower at the top of the stem.

The life cycle of these plants is abbreviated: they grow rapidly, bloom, seed, and die within a few days, sometimes within a few hours. The life of the blossoms is usually shorter—seldom more than two to four hours. There are flowers that will grow, bloom, seed, and die within twenty-four to thirty-six hours. These herbaceous plants vary in height from two millimeters to forty-five centimeters (one-sixteenth of an inch to eighteen inches, respectively).

The second of the two general types includes

shrubs with tough, woody, or wiry stems. These plants live for many years and can survive prolonged drought if they are well-established. Many have leaves that are not readily seen and will often appear to be no more than a few old dead sticks or a tangled, wiry mass. The life of the blossoms on these plants is as brief as those herbaceous blossoms. In height, the plants vary from four centimeters to sixty centimeters (one and one-half inches to twenty-three inches, respectively).

These plants survive by special adaptations to desert conditions; there is an evolutionary advantage in reducing the surface area of leaves, stems, and other parts of plants growing in arid climates. This reduces the amount of water lost through transpiration, so that under conditions of high temperature and scant water supply, small plants have a decided advantage over those with larger leaves. Furthermore, very small plants use less energy to bring about germination of seeds before the available water supply is exhausted. In contrast, large annual plants may be killed by drought before they can even reach the flowering stage, let alone cast their seed.

Many of the plants have leaves that are covered with a mass of hairlike filaments. All their leaves are tough; some are pulpy inside, while their exteriors are covered with a waxlike substance similar to that

of cacti. Some plants are covered with what looks like crystallized sugar. The leaves of some are buried shallowly in the sand with only the stem exposed. All of these adaptations retard the loss of moisture, allowing the plants to retain it long enough to complete their life cycle.

Far out in the desert, these little flowers are difficult to find, but to search for them makes their discovery all the more satisfying. So for a period of ten years (1971 through 1980), my wife, Katharine, and I traveled the arid West in search of the elusive flowers. We made thirty expeditions, each of from fifteen to thirty-four days, and covered more than 75,000 miles through twenty-five deserts. After 694 days of travel, 101 different miniflowers had been photographed for the first time. A portion of that collection follows.

The identifying characteristics for each flower are listed in the captions under or opposite each image. For ease of identification, the family name is listed first, followed by the generic and specific (Latin) names, the approximate diameter, and a common name, if one has been designated. Flowers larger than four millimeters are not considered true miniflowers. Where a question mark appears, exact identification was not possible due to poor samples or lack of complete taxonomic criteria.

Bean, *Lotus humistratus,* 2.60 mm

"There is an eloquence to their forms which stirs the imagination with a singular power, and kindles in the mind of the dullest observer a glowing response."

CLARENCE DUTTON

In 1971, on the lip of Lunar Crater in south-central Nevada, about 100 miles southwest of Ely, I noticed a fungus approximately three inches tall growing out of the rock and sand. I had always thought fungi (toadstools, mushrooms, and the like) grew only in shady damp places. Yet here was one in, of all places, the arid desert of Nevada.

I had been photographing fungi for years and could not pass up the chance of getting a picture of this one, bravely erect, with its black hair neatly parted in the middle. While photographing it, I accidentally dropped the lens hood. Leaning down to pick it up, I noticed that the ground was covered with tiny plants. On the plants were white specks that were flowers. So I took a picture using the full set of extension rings that give a reproduction ratio of 1:1. In other words, the image on the film would be the exact size of the plant and flower.

When the film was developed and the image projected on the screen at home, I was amazed to see an exquisite white flower about 1.5 millimeters in diameter with six petals striped with pink, complete with pink-tipped stamens and a yellow pistil. There had been thousands of tiny flowers on the ground that we had walked over many times without ever seeing. It was then that I decided to have a go at finding and photographing these flowers, and set about acquiring the necessary equipment and learn-

Buckwheat, *Eriogonum microthecum*, 2.33 mm

Buckwheat, *Eriogonum corymbosum*, 3.75 mm

ing how to use it.

I was unable to find anyone who could tell me about high-magnification photography in the field. This lack of existing knowledge was not encouraging, but after consultation with many photography experts, I bought the equipment they recommended with the expectation that I would learn how to use it the hard way. Katharine and I then took off into the deserts with no idea of where to look for or how to find another miniflower.

We drove for three weeks and almost 2,500 miles before we found a flower in Snow Canyon in the Escalante Desert; we located it only by the faint shadow its thin, wiry stem cast on the sand. My struggles with this flower and the new equipment quickly reminded me that I was indeed a novice at this kind of photography. I learned that I needed much more and better equipment in order to devise and perfect techniques of photographing flowers where they grow, or in the camper if weather was bad. My experimenting paid off.

Winter was coming on and we would make no more trips that year, so I spent the entire season photographing pin heads and tiny bits of white, blue, yellow, and red embroidery yarns. Two electronic flashes were used, each placed at different and precise distances from the "flower" to produce soft shadows. The flash positioning, which controls the exposure, was determined by trial and took into account each of the four colors, each of eight lens magnifications, and each of three degrees of exposure (over, standard, and under) to compensate for the unknown variations in film speed.

After thousands of measurements and calculations, the expenditure of 720 slides (36 rolls of film), and eye strain, I had a set of exposure tables that told me exactly how far each flash was to be placed from any color flower to take the kinds of photographs I wanted. In these tables, there are 192 distance figures noted in both centimeters and inches.

The entire system is built around a 35-millimeter single lens reflex camera with a lockup mirror and a matte viewing screen. I use a 140-millimeter adjustable bellows with a swivel head and a built-in focusing rack that is augmented with 50 millimeters of extention tubes—190 millimeters in all. The lens is a 35-millimeter wide-angle reversed with a special hood to avoid flash flare and blowing sand. With this equipment, I can achieve a reproduction ratio of eight to one (an 8x magnification). The entire photographic equipment assembly—shot bags, mirrors, tripods, high-intensity viewing light for inside photography, and other miscellaneous items—totaled thirty-four separate gadgets, some of them specially made, and all of them essential. With such a system, I developed two successful methods of photographing the flowers.

In the first method, I use direct sunlight supplemented with two mirrors. The sun is at its maximum and the air is at its quietest between 11 a.m.

and 2 p.m.—two essentials for successfully photographing the flowers, since strong, natural light is desirable and the slightest breeze will cause a miniature flower to toss about like a palm tree in a hurricane. It is also during these hours that the ground and air temperatures soar; lying prone in sand, rocks, thorns, and cactus spines has little to recommend it. But this method produces the best pictures and is the only one that can be used when the plant is too fragile to be moved.

The second method is used when the sky is overcast and I cannot get enough natural light, when the wind is blowing, or when there is some other reason why the flower cannot be photographed in its natural setting. With this method, however, the plant must have a tough stem. After setting up the equipment in the camper, I carefully dig the plant out of the ground and place it in a glass full of sand and water; I then dash inside with it and work as rapidly as possible to photograph the plant before it dies. Sometimes it dies while being photographed.

Neither of these methods is easier than the other, and with each, about three hours are required to set up the equipment and take a roll of twenty exposures. I always take a full roll of a single flower with the hope that at least one picture will be acceptable. There is so much that can go wrong—and frequently does—that I want a good margin for error. This practice has saved me many times. It takes another hour to stow away the gear and prepare the specimens for pressing, drying, and identification.

There was only one concern remaining: how to convince the viewers of the photographs just how tiny the flowers actually are. Without a relative size comparison, the miniflowers would appear to be as large as sunflowers. The solution was to include in each picture the very point of the smallest seamstress's pin or the head of an ordinary kitchen match. (Sometimes, however, I became so involved that I forgot to make certain that the pin was in the picture.)

With the particulars of photographing the miniflowers out of the way, we were ready to begin our journey. Little did we realize that we would become so involved in the world of these tiny flowers that we would spend the next nine years in pursuit of them. In our search, we followed mere tracks into the most remote parts of deserts from Oregon to Mexico, sometimes finding ourselves ninety miles from the nearest surfaced road.

The vehicle in which we traveled deserves mention because without it our adventures would have been either impossible or suicidal. After forty-five years of traveling in the desert, I knew what we needed in a rig that could take us virtually anywhere and bring us back in comfort and with some degree of safety. I had a camper custom made and permanently mounted on a specially assembled pickup

Borage, *Cryptantha gracilis,* 0.90 mm

truck of massive strength and power. The entire unit was painted desert green and brown, two spare tires were mounted in front of the radiator, and a flashing beacon was mounted on the roof. The long windows could be removed and cameras mounted inside in case a blind was needed for photographing wildlife. It was completely self-contained and carried enough supplies for ten days and 300 miles of off-road travel.

"All the world was before me and every day was a holiday, so it did not seem important to which one of the world's wildernesses I first should wander."

JOHN MUIR

In June and July of 1973, we traveled through southwestern Utah, stopping at Coral Pink Sand Dunes State Park, Zion National Park, and Cedar Breaks National Park. Zion is far more beautiful than can ever be described with pen or picture. The colors—red, ochre, burnt umber—of the near-vertical walls of this narrow canyon are intensified by the lush green vegetation that grows on the banks of the Virgin River. In some places, the walls are streaked with vertical black bands that have been formed by water seeps hundreds of feet above the canyon floor; along these seeps are vines,

Bean, *Astragalus tegetarius,* 3.50 mm

flowers, and small bushes, growing wherever they can find a crack in the rock.

When the desert sun came up over the canyon walls in the morning, it struck with some authority, forewarning that the day would be hot, with no clouds to temper the searing rays. It reminded me of the first time I had come to this place in 1929; the roads were dirt and there was no traffic. When I brought Katharine to Zion in 1932, the roads were still dirt and not a visitor could be found. On this visit, however, there were hordes of people and traffic was somewhat of a problem.

We parked in the shade of some giant cottonwood trees, where Katharine assembled her camera

Phlox, *Ipomopsis pumila,* 5.10 mm

equipment and asked if I wanted to join her on a hike. There was a short path leading to an observation point from which one could get a good view of the river and the surrounding cliffs of the canyon. I agreed, intending to take down one of our lounge chairs to just lie in the shade and watch the people.

We had gone no more than one hundred feet, when I noticed a thin, scraggly patch of dusty green in the middle of the path. It was small—only about three inches wide and a foot long—but I had a strong feeling that it should be investigated. I went back to the truck and got my hand glass; then, on hands and knees, my nose almost touching the ground, I carefully inspected the patch and found it full of very tiny pink flowers hidden among the leaves. The individual plants were only about four millimeters in height. They could not be seen when standing upright, but there they were, blooming in their full glory and being stepped on by countless feet.

I charged into action like a firehorse upon hearing the bell and forgot all about Katharine. A glance at my watch told me the sun was near its zenith—prime time for photographing. I had to hurry, knowing the life of a miniflower is seldom more than two or three hours. After about twenty minutes and three trips to the truck for equipment, I had everything set up and was lying on the ground cloth, propped up on my elbows, and peering through the viewfinder.

Now the real work began. Because of the high magnification of the camera, I could see only a part of the flower in a space measuring three by five millimeters and about sixteen-hundreths of a millimeter in depth; it was a major task to maneuver the camera in three directions to even find the blossom. Then, if the angle was not right, I had to move the equipment and start again.

Finally, I located the four pink petals in the viewfinder and a surge of pure joy rushed through me. No one had ever seen the flower as clearly as I could see it and the picture would reveal even more of its crisp detail. I glanced at my watch: forty-five minutes had elapsed and I had not even started photographing.

The sun, blazing down from a cloudless sky, was not casting enough light on the flower, so I carefully adjusted two small mirrors to provide additional light and again looked into the camera. The flower was gone! What had happened? After close examination, I found that the bracket supporting the camera and affixed to the tripod leg had slipped under the combined weight of the camera, bellows, focusing rack, and stabilizing shot bag, which I used to dampen any vibration that might be caused by the shutter.

I readjusted and tightened everything and noted that the flower was now brighter in the viewfinder. Everything was ready. I made the fine focusing adjustments and closed down the aperture to take an exposure reading, but while I was doing this, the needle on the light meter suddenly dropped. Again I opened the aperture and looked into the camera, but no flower was there. The camera had drooped again and there was no way that I could detect its movement without looking into it. A shift of only one millimeter threw the whole set-up out of alignment.

Again, I readjusted and tightened everything, this time using both hands, but the bracket still would not hold. I roundly cursed the store that had sold me the equipment while I pondered what to do. My elbows were killing me (the ground cloth was not much of a cushion), and my neck and shoulders were stiff. The whole situation looked bad.

After a bit, I placed a small stone under the focusing rack, but that didn't work very well because I could not make the vertical adjustment. Then I looked for and found a dead stick about an inch in diameter, whittled a wedge, and placed it under the focusing rack. It worked fine and I was in business again.

After a few minutes, I had once again brought the image of the flower into the viewfinder. By then the flower had moved to follow the sun, and I had to move the equipment and begin again. Another twenty minutes had gone by and I still had no pictures. After adjusting the sun mirrors, I went to work. I would usually talk aloud to myself to avoid forgetting a step in the procedure: cock the shutter,

Vervain, *Verbena bracteata,* 3.00 mm

fine focus, stop down the aperture, read the exposure meter, adjust the shutter speed, lock up the camera mirror, set the self-timer, shoot. Then take three more pictures, unlock the camera mirror, open the aperture, and look to make sure the flower was still in focus.

The flower was bobbing about as though in a hurricane. I did not even feel the air movement that was causing so much commotion in the plant's miniature world. The gusts lasted for a few moments only, and I continued to take pictures, hoping that the flower would stand still for at least one shot. The hurricane had thrown the flower slightly out of focus, so again I cocked the shutter, adjusted the fine focus, closed down the aperture, read the exposure meter, adjusted the shutter, locked the mirror up, set the self-timer, snapped the picture. Then another three shots and so on and so on.

There were more hurricanes and the flower shifted with the sun, but I was able to compensate for it this time with bellows adjustments. Finally the roll of twenty pictures had been taken and I lay back for a few moments, totally exhausted. I looked at my watch: 3:05 p.m. It had taken me three hours and thirty-five minutes to photograph one flower. I wondered that the flower had lasted that long.

Back at the truck, I found that Katharine had been there for about two hours and had stood watching me for a short time. I had not noticed her, nor anyone else for that matter. Badly dehydrated, I had to drink slowly to avoid cramps. Under my shirt, my sunburned skin was extremely tender. I resolved then and there to give up photography forever. While I relaxed on the bed sipping wine and water, Katharine told me about her efforts and about what she had seen from the truck.

While I had been lying on the path, scores of people had passed on their way to the lookout. They would be striding along the path talking and laughing when suddenly they would see me and come to a full stop. After deciding that I was probably not dangerous, they would circle me in a cautious manner as though not to take any chances, stop again and look back, and continue on their way. At times when the foot traffic was heavy, those going and coming completely surrounded me.

When they saw Katharine sitting and reading in the camper, some would come to the door and ask her what I was doing. She would explain that I was photographing a flower, to which they would reply, with an expression suggesting that both Katharine and I had lost our minds, that they saw no flowers. Katharine would patiently explain that the flowers were so small that it was almost impossible to see them without a magnifying glass. On hearing this, some would stomp about and peer closely at the ground, and a few would come back to verify that I was indeed photographing a flower. After being reassured, they would walk away muttering to themselves that now they had seen everything.

By the time I had collected my specimens and put away my equipment, most of the people had left the area; there were fewer cars on the road as we drove slowly down the canyon. We returned to our place in the campground, lay back in the chairs with comforting drinks, and watched the evening shadows creep up the canyon walls.

When the ranger came by to collect our camping fee, he looked at me and the truck intently and finally recognized me as the man who had been lying on the ground in the upper canyon for most of the day. I admitted that I was the one and told him what I had been doing. He had never heard of miniflowers before and was fascinated with the subject. He inquired about my tolerance for the heat, and when I told him that it had been a little warm, he went on to tell me that it had been 105 degrees in the canyon and that I had created all sorts of excitement in the community; all afternoon people had been telephoning and stopping at headquarters to report a strange man lying on the ground.

It was still warm when Katharine started dinner—close to 100 degrees in the camper—and I began to check the cameras and prepare them for whatever we might find the next day. I went over Katharine's camera and then looked at mine. I was struck with a cold chill. The film speed adjustment—the ASA—had been knocked out of its proper setting! Every picture on the roll would be ruined! I must have let out a cry of anguish because Katharine dropped whatever it was that she held in her hand and asked what had happened. When I told her, she was appropriately sympathetic.

It is imperative that the camera be accurately adjusted to the speed of the film; if it is not, the shift in colors is nothing less than catastrophic. I had done everything possible to ensure accurate color exposures—adjusted the camera to a master light meter, made test exposures, refrigerated the film—and now this. There are times when something goes wrong that one can relieve the tension by shouting or swearing or stomping about, but this was far too serious for that. We just sat there in despair. My thought processes came to a full stop and stayed there until Katharine provided another drink. When I returned to consciousness, I decided that I would go back to the little patch of vegetation and do it all over again—if I could find another flower.

The next morning we arose without much enthusiasm. I had spent a good part of the night trying to figure out how the ASA adjustment had been moved and decided that it must have happened when I was wrestling with the faulty leg bracket. There was no reason to be back in the field before 11:00 a.m., because the flowers would not be open before then; for that matter, they might not be there at all.

When we arrived at the flower site, I immediately took my hand glass and walked down the path I had worked on the day before. The patch of plants had diminished in size; most were dying, having completed their life cycle, but a few still remained. I searched anxiously among them for more blossoms and found three that were starting to open. Knowing that this was possibly my last chance for years, I was determined to be extra cautious.

As quickly as possible, I assembled the camera gear at the site. The sun beat down with a vengeance—it was going to be hotter than it had been

Bean, *Hosackia strigosa,* 2.50 mm, Bird's Foot Trefoil

the day before. This time I knew where to place the tripod to compensate for the movement of the flower as it followed the sun, and I still had my wooden wedge. By the time everything was ready, the flowers were fully open; I selected the best one of three and went to work. It took me just as long to find the flower in the viewfinder and focus on it as it had before; then I started the countdown, following each step of the procedure with the utmost care.

Each time I cocked the shutter I worried that the camera might have moved despite the fact that it and the tripod were weighed down with twelve pounds of shot bags, and the adjustments were as tight as I could make them. Again, I was oblivious to everything that was going on around me and talked aloud to myself as I went through the details of the procedure. When the roll was finished, I lay back for a few moments, then sat up and looked at my watch. It had taken two hours and forty minutes.

It was not until then that I realized my elbows were killing me and the top of my head felt as though it had been fried. (I can't wear a hat when doing this work because it gets in the way and blocks out the sun at the wrong time; what little hair I do have is no protection from the western sun.)

I noticed a man and woman standing nearby; from the puzzled expression on their faces, I could see that they had been watching and listening to me for more than a few minutes. He finally asked what I was doing, and I told them about the flowers. They walked closer and looked carefully at the little patch of rapidly fading green but could not see the flowers, so I moved the tripod and handed him the hand glass, pointing out where the flower was hiding. Down on his hands and knees, he soon found the blossom and let out a burst of amazement, then invited his wife to take a look. She was not interested.

All this time, Katharine had been sitting in the truck with her fingers crossed and occasionally knocking on wood to keep away any bad luck. Once more, she patiently answered the questions of curious observers.

Having captured the flowers on film and feeling content about seeing Zion Canyon, we decided to move on and continue our search elsewhere. We had a lot of land to cover, and with the temperature rising, there was no point in dallying at any one place. Coral Sands is about forty miles east of Zion, is at a higher elevation, and is generally much cooler; because it was an undeveloped state park on a dirt road, there would be few, if any, people. So we packed our things and turned toward the sun.

The highway going east from Zion climbs a steep switchback and enters a long tunnel built into a vertical red rock cliff. The bore of the tunnel is not very wide and was built before the advent of the huge RVs, so I was a little apprehensive about confronting one of these in the bowels of the mountain.

Sure enough, we met one and as we crept through the tunnel, scraped the wall and knocked a rearview mirror askew. It was close, very close, and I imagined the consequences if two rigs got jammed together when trying to pass. We arrived at Coral Sands late in the afternoon, just in time for Katharine to have the best light for photographing, and found the campground among juniper trees beside the dunes. After we had picked our site, we drove back up the road and found a better camera angle.

Coral Sands is unbelievable—strictly a picture postcard of the most garish kind. It is hard to believe that these colors have been here, unchanged, for thousands of years. The dunes are not large—a little more than a mile long and less than a quarter-mile wide—and are located in the bottom of a shallow valley formed by low, red earth mountains on which dusty, dark green junipers grow in modest profusion. Along the base of the coral pink dunes, clumps of large, brilliant yellow flowers were blooming. Overhead, the sky was a crisp marine blue. Each color complemented the others to produce a scene that was nothing less than spectacular. The valley opened to the south, and we could see over and beyond the lower red mountains and their trees to the high northern desert of Arizona.

When we arrived at our place in the campground, a welcoming committee was on hand to greet us—five or six domestic ducks, rather surprising since every drop of water used here must be

Mint, *Salvia reflexa,* 3.14 mm, Sage

21

hauled from miles away. The ranger station was closed, and there were no other rigs there, so we and the ducks had the place all to ourselves. The air was perfect, and we lay in the chairs until the stars came out. It was absolutely quiet except for a duck's occasional soft quacking.

The next morning, we started rather late and with no idea of where we were going, but by the time we reached the highway, we had decided to go on to Cedar Breaks. The road climbed steadily and it was not long before we saw snow covering the ground in the forest. As we approached the lodge, we skirted a big meadow saturated with dandelions. At that elevation, above 10,000 feet, the growing season is very short and the flowers were wasting no time. We didn't stay there long—an icy wind was blowing and we decided to seek a more temperate clime.

We were not at all reluctant to start west across the Escalante Desert. The sun promised that it would be another hot day. When we started climbing into the mountains of Nevada, we pulled off the road and stopped for a break. Immediately upon stepping from the truck, Katharine found a miniflower. I leveled the truck to ensure that the refrigerator would continue to function, assembled my gear, and went to work on the flower. It was a beautiful little thing, much like a white orchid. Everything went smoothly, and by the time I had finished photographing, it was still early in the afternoon.

We camped that night at a cool 6,800 feet, and the next morning I found what I was sure would be a miniflower when it opened. Like an anxious father-to-be, I must have inspected it every three minutes for the next hour, and when I saw that it would indeed be a miniflower, I set up the equipment with haste and was ready when the last of its five tiny petals of the palest pink unfolded. Again everything went well, and in less than three hours I had the pictures, the specimen, and the gear stowed away.

Later that day, when we stopped for gas, we met a couple from the East Coast who were shocked and dismayed by the desert, the heat, and the distances. When they asked where they could find the forests, I was a little taken aback by the question. I explained to them that the national forests shown on their Nevada map are not as they envisioned them—stands of green, leafy trees and a carpet of soft grass. Here the forests consist of widely spaced, gnarled, low junipers, cacti, some sage and greasewood, sand, and rocks. Sometimes the trees are so small that it is questionable whether they are trees or shrubs. There are some sparse forests of pine, fir, and aspen near the tips of the peaks, but the mountains are so steep that it is almost impossible to get to them except on foot or horseback. I suggested that they forget the forests.

On our way west toward Tonopah, we were in familiar territory. We had been on this road many times; the first had been forty years before when it

Great Nevada Desert

was just dirt. There were no bridges across the dry washes and there had been nothing along its 170 miles of raw desert—not even a telephone pole. At that time the state ran a patrol over it every day or two to pick up stragglers. Now it was not much better except that the road was paved and there were two forlorn gas stations—their paint faded and peeling, their signs blown askew by horrendous winds, some battered oil drums scattered about, and piles of empty oil cans strewn with reckless abandon.

This was but a small part of the Great Nevada Desert—huge, foreboding, hot, empty, and dangerous. The sand and rock, sparse vegetation, and grass so thin and burned out that it could scarcely be seen, all seemed to be the same color—ochre lightly mixed with burnt umber. Even the sky had a brassy look, and the sun was furious. The road crossed range after range of low nude mountains, and from the top of one range, the road could be seen stretching endlessly to the next.

About halfway to Tonopah, there is one range that is different and stands in stark contrast to the monochrome of the terrain. It is black. The base of the rounded volcanic ash hills are streaked with yellow sand, blown upon them by the sandstorms that lash this area. The sides of the cinder cones are streaked with deep red, looking as though it has not been long since these mountains were aflame. It was in this range, at Lunar Crater, south of the highway, that we had accidentally found our first miniature flower a little more than two years before. It had been earlier in the year (June), and at the higher elevation, much of the new growth still remained. Now it looked as though nothing green had been there, ever. Anyone who has not seen this transformation of the desert cannot quite believe it.

I noticed two lenticular clouds forming across the horizon to the west early that afternoon. This type of cloud is a positive warning of high winds, and from the rapidity with which they were building, I knew that trouble was ahead. Before we started again, we tightly closed all the windows and ventilators but knew that it would really not do much good because the sand would get into everything. Soon we could see the storm approaching—a gigantic, rolling wall of sand, dust, and flying brush that extended hundreds of feet skyward; it hit us head-on with a shrieking roar. The truck, staggered by the blow, slowed to less than 30 mph and lurched violently as I wrestled with the wheel to keep it on the road. A lesser rig could easily have been turned over.

Hour after hour we battled the wind and sand, up over one range and down again toward the next. The storm showed no signs of abating—in fact at times it seemed to become even more fierce. The refrigerator flame blew out; no flame, no refrigeration. I must have relighted it a half-dozen times before I gave up in despair.

About five or six miles before we came to Tonopah, a road from the north intersected our route, and I took it in an effort to get out of the storm. Now the wind hit us broadside and the truck tried to take evasive action by attempting to dart across the road or out into the desert. I reduced our speed even more and we reeled down the road for about twenty miles before the wind began to subside. It was late in the evening when we found a place to stop in a small, barren, and unused campground across the road from a maintenance station. Ely was 268 miles behind us, and we had seen two half-dead gas stations and the remnants of a ghost town on the side of a hill. Sand covered everything in the camper; on the floor there was even a small riffle of sand that extended six or seven feet from the door.

"Oh but the desert is glorious now, with marching clouds in the blue sky, and cool winds blowing. The smell of sage is sweet in my nostrils, and the luring trail leads onward."

EVERETT RUESS

We were looking for miniflowers along the Carrol Pass road in Nevada, which had been part of Highway 50 but was now virtually abandoned, and saw no cars and no flowers. I had hoped to find some flowers at the higher elevation—about 7,000 feet—but the whole country was burnt to a crisp by the summer sun, and it was obvious that there had been little snow or rain there during the winter. Along the bottoms of the arroyos, the aspen were still green and flourishing.

The ground had been leveled to provide fill for the highway when it was built years before. Now it

Pink, *Stellaria nitens,* 7.00 mm, Star of Nevada

was covered with sparse, short, dry grass and weeds but offered a beautiful evening view of a broad, shallow valley in the Great Nevada Desert. The air was cool and pleasant; we decided to stay put.

As usual we started looking for miniflowers. Katharine immediately found one; then I found one, and both of us were crawling about on our hands and knees. We found two more. That made four: two white, one pink, and one blue, all within a few feet of the truck. We had driven into a veritable flower garden. I crawled all over the place with my hand glass, then marked a small area in the sand and started counting. When I reached 150, I stopped counting and estimated that there were easily between 150 and 200 flowers growing on every square

foot of this ground; all were grandly displaying their glory for the enjoyment of everyone, but only Katharine and I were there to see them.

It was too late in the afternoon to start photographing, and there were so many flowers that we did not bother to stake out any of them. The next morning I had everything ready when they started to open and found that their number had diminished considerably. As soon as I had finished with the first, a white flower slightly more than one millimeter in its full diameter, I started on the second flower—a bit larger than the first but also white. I worked as rapidly as possible; even so, it took me a little more than four hours to photograph the two.

In the meantime, Katharine looked for the pink and the blue flowers but could not find them— neither could I. I strongly suspected that these two were ephemeral. In any case, they were gone, perhaps not to reappear for five, ten, or as many as thirty years. The white flowers were rapidly disappearing, and I was certain that no trace of them would be found the next day. There was no point in staying longer, so after I had stowed away my gear and pressed the specimens, we started down the road.

By the time we were out of the mountains, it was afternoon and long lines of whirlwinds began

Bean, *Astragalus nuttalii,* 2.75 mm

to dance across the endless dry sage flats and the road ahead. They carry a surprising force and can easily upset a high rig such as ours. We settled down to a long grind toward our destination, which was about fifty miles west of Ely, and hoped that we would get there before nightfall.

It was almost sundown when we turned off the highway onto a sheep camp road. We followed it for several miles as it wound among the sage, finally ending behind a low, rounded hill. This spot, one of our favorites, offered an unlimited view down and across a shallow valley to the juniper-covered mountains beyond. When we stopped, absolute serenity pervaded the valley, the shadows lengthened, and darkness enveloped the land. The moon hung above the eastern horizon, and far down the valley we could faintly hear the coyotes sing.

While exploring the area the following morning, I found another miniflower only a few inches from one of the truck's front wheels. This took me by surprise because the vegetation everywhere was dead. Even the sage was dry and brittle, and there were no signs of little rodents, birds, or insects— just this one dusty, half-dead tiny plant with one blossom looking up at me like the well-washed face of a grubby child. Its five pink petals had a full span of no more than three millimeters. Indeed, this little flower displayed its tenacity by blooming in a severe drought, and I vowed to take the best picture of

Phlox, *Gilia leptomeria,* 3.00 mm

it that I could. Little did I realize that it would create all kinds of interest in the scientific community.*

While lying in the sand and rocks, I became aware that this would be another hot day and that the sun would be particularly severe when we got into the southern part of the Sevier Desert in Utah, which is about 2,000 feet lower than where we

*The botanists at Stanford University and the University of California at Berkeley had no record of this flower. What they do in cases such as this (and there were several others) is send the specimen to those botanists who specialize in identification—places such as the New York Botanical Society, the Smithsonian Institution, the St. Louis Botanical Gardens, and others. In this case, the specimen was sent from one place to another until it was identified; it took several months.

Phlox, *Gilia latifolia,* 7.50 mm

were. I was not wrong; the temperature went straight up. Shimmering heat waves rose from the asphalt that stretched endlessly ahead, and a huge mirage lifted the mountains above a vast dry lake to the south. Dust devils, in long chorus lines, tripped their way across the sands all around us, making everything an earth yellow. We eventually arrived in Delta, Utah, and stopped for the night.

We were well through the mountains of the Wasatch Plateau the following day when we pulled off onto a sheep camp road that led to another of our favorite sites. It is high, about 8,500 feet, and set in green grass growing under quaking aspen trees. During the summer, this is sheep country—broad

grassy meadows filled with flowers between aspen-, fir-, and pine-covered mountains. We wandered about, taking in all we could, when Katharine called to me that she had found a miniflower.

Immediately I went into action, and sure enough, there was a small patch of miniflowers. These were white with yellow stamen and so very small that, even though they were growing on slender stems about ten inches tall, they could scarcely be seen. Katharine stood there while I got a stake with a ribbon attached to mark the location. (We have learned the hard way that when we find a flower it must be staked out so we can find it again.) Everything went perfectly: the light was good, the grass was soft, it was not hot, and the equipment was cooperative. In two hours and fifty minutes the job was complete.

It was still early in the day, so we decided to follow the road and see a little more of this high country; if the road ended, we could always find a good place to park for the night and return the way we had come. Although the road had never been graded, it was in good shape. It wound about over the tops of the mountains as it followed the grass that sheep grazed upon. The altimeter told us that we were near 10,000 feet most of the time, and the vistas from the high points were impressive. To the north, west, and south we could see green, gentle

Waterleaf, *Phacelia rotundifolia,* 4.75 mm

mountain tops rising above the plateau to almost 12,000 feet; to the east we could see the vast reaches of the San Raphael Desert with its lavender sands, looking hot and fearsome. After many miles, the road started to descend into a small, lush, green valley where it joined a single lane paved road, and I was able to determine where we were.

At the minute town of Fremont, the road widened to two narrow lanes and wound around small farms that had been established by Mormon settlers more than one hundred years before. Because of the altitude, about 7,000 feet, the choice of crops is rather limited—potatoes, some grain, and alfalfa to feed sheep and cattle through the long winters. The Fremont River, with willows and cottonwoods lining its banks, is small here because it is not far from its headwaters in the mountains.

In about twenty miles, we passed through four delightful little towns, their streets lined with ancient cottonwood trees that had grown to an immense size. Every building was neat and well cared for. The houses, with their sparkling windows, had clipped lawns, and we saw a few women in sunbonnets working in their vegetable and flower gardens. The atmosphere was one of withdrawn quiet.

The road continued to descend, and suddenly we were in a desert of red earth and rock with little vegetation. As we rounded a bench, we saw in the distance to the east a towering cliff of dark red sandstone that extended across the horizon. In the

Buckwheat, *Eriogonum thomasii,* 2.00 mm

late afternoon sun, it seemed to glow like red-hot iron, its color intensified by the green on the mountain tops on either side of us. The place was Capitol Reef, the northern part of a gigantic barrier that extends almost one hundred miles south to the Colorado River.

It was late in the day when we turned off the road and parked in the grass of an old orchard at the bottom of a narrow canyon where red cliffs rise a thousand feet or more. It is here that the Fremont River has cut through the reef on its way east to join the Dirty Devil River in the desert. This place has been one of our favorites since we "discovered" it many years before; we had gone to some trouble to get to it by driving through the desert over seventy-five or eighty miles of primitive dirt road. At that time, few people had ever heard of Capitol Reef, and I had learned about it only by chance.

It is now Capitol Reef National Park, smaller than the Grand Canyon, which it far surpasses in color, and with adjoining country to the south containing some of the most dramatic and savage terrain on this earth. The entire area is composed of sedimentary rock of various kinds. Within the park, formations of sandstone, limestone, and shale have been exposed by water and wind erosion to a depth of more than 9,000 feet. Each of the stratum is a different color: red, gray, golden yellow, white, green, lavender, black, chocolate brown, and all shades in between. When they are wet from rain, the effect is breathtaking. The erosion of each of these stratum causes the formation of unusual landforms: domes, from which the reef gets it name; arches and natural bridges; or hollows, which become pools when it rains. The variety seems to be endless.

After a leisurely breakfast the next morning, we walked up the Fremont River and enjoyed the sights and smells of green grass, bowing willows, and rushing water. (Water seems to smell different in the desert.) We didn't go very far, maybe a half-mile, before the hiking began to get difficult, and thinking that we didn't need that much exercise, started back. We had almost reached the campground when I found what looked like a miniflower growing on a long stalk, so I cut it off and returned to the truck to examine it. It was indeed a miniflower, pale blue and delicate.

I could not photograph this flower where it was growing because it was in dense brush next to the rushing stream. Wanting the use of natural light, though, I pondered the problem for a few moments, then set up the camera on a picnic table and asked Katharine to guard it while I found and cut another flower, stuffed its stem down into a drinking glass full of sand and water, and went to work. Within three hours, I had a roll of pictures, and the gear and specimen were stowed away.

In the meantime, all sorts of people strolled by, stopped to see what I was doing, but were too polite to come closer—or maybe they thought it best to stay a safe distance from a man who did nothing but spend hours photographing a glass full of sand. During all this, Katharine was keeping a clear distance to avoid having to answer questions.

"Whatsoever might be bold and striking would at first seem only grotesque."

CLARENCE DUTTON

I had noticed on the park map a place called Cathedral Valley, just inside the northern boundary of Capitol Reef. We thought it might be an interesting place to look for miniflowers, but the only access was a four-wheel-drive road. This connoted all sorts of things, primarily that I had better investigate before we got into something that we could not get out of. So we drove to park headquarters to make inquiries.

The first thing the rangers wanted to know was why I wanted to go to Cathedral Valley. When I told them about my search for flowers, they were so interested that I spent the next twenty minutes tell-

Spurge, *Chamaesyce setiloba,* 2.83 mm, La Golondrina

ing them about miniflowers. The rangers had never heard of them. They also inquired about the vehicle I was driving, and when they learned that it was not equipped with four-wheel drive, they were dubious about the whole idea. I took them to look over the truck, and after their inspection, they finally agreed that it was powerful enough to make the trip.

Back in the office, the rangers discussed the best route for me to take. If I went in from the south, the closest access, I would first have to ford the Fremont River, which has a solid bottom but was running high and swift. Moreover, the far bank was abruptly steep, and I might have to wade across with a shovel and dig it down to be on the safe side. Then, about six or seven miles beyond the Fremont, I

would reach the Pinto Hills; but these would give me no trouble unless it rained. If it did rain, we would be in deep trouble because the truck would not be able to move, and we would be there until the ground dried. These bentonite (clay) hills are the consistency of mayonnaise when wet and just as slippery. Beyond the Pinto Hills six or seven miles, I would come to a wide, dry wash filled with soft sand, which had the tendency to trap any cars that tried to cross it and sometimes bogged down four-wheel drives. Aside from these obstacles, the road was easily passable as far as the wash; beyond that, no one knew the condition, since it had been a couple of weeks and several thunderstorms since anyone had been back that way.

They suggested I go into the valley from the west side, which is the long way around, but the access road would give me less trouble, at least until I got into the valley itself. The western route goes over a range of mountains and is within the jurisdiction of the U.S. Forest Service, which takes care of road maintenance, so the rangers called the forest service office to ask about the condition of the road. We didn't learn much, except that the road was solid and passable—at least it had been a couple of months before.

To reach the western access road to Cathedral Valley, we had to retrace our steps almost to the place where we had first encountered the paved road coming off the high mountain. The rangers had given me good directions, and we easily found the turnoff that we wanted.

The beginning segment was paved and immediately started to climb across the range, but after only a short distance, it turned into a grass-covered track. As the grade became steeper, the engine began to rumble in a defiant manner. The track wound through quaking aspen, which grew along the side of the hill, and soon we were on top of a rise at about 9,000 feet. We couldn't see much except the tall white trunks of the aspen and their leaves—silver on the underside and green on the top—which shimmer and rustle with the slightest movement of air. Overhead, a few fleecy clouds drifted in a quiet sky.

We stopped for a few moments to look beyond the crest and saw the road drop steeply before disappearing altogether in the trees. We then continued over the summit and followed the descending road as it wound among the aspen, some of which were dead and leaning so close over the path that I had to carefully judge the clearance to avoid snagging them. If one of these had been a little closer to the road, it would have meant backing up to the crest and turning around. We descended so rapidly that we could see the hands of the altimeter move. Suddenly we were out of the aspen and into brush; then, about a half-mile farther, we were in the desert on a high bench sparsely covered with juniper trees.

Figwort, *Collinsia parviflora,* 4.25 mm

39

From the edge of this bench, we looked down upon Cathedral Valley. It is not very big—only a few miles long and maybe a mile or so wide—but it is breathtaking in its color and grandeur. Millions of years of erosion have exposed the strata and carved the walls that rise hundreds of feet above the red earth floor. The vertical face of the stratum at the base is dark red-brown, followed successively by layers of a lighter reddish brown, chocolate brown, white, black, pale lavender, and burnt orange. The towering formations are topped with a white cap-rock, which is broken and gives the impression of battlements on a castle wall.

On the floor of red sand are the formations that give this valley its name—enormous gothic cathedrals, their fluted reddish brown walls supported by buttresses separated from the steep peaked roofs of white by a trim of chocolate brown. One can almost see the high vaulted ceilings and the tall narrow stained glass windows. There are others that are smaller and of the modern A-frame and pyramid designs. Tall, sparse grass, scattered sage and brush, and a few junipers complete the scene. It all seems unreal.

Driving down into the valley, I was not reassured by the track, which abruptly dipped over the edge of the valley wall and followed a very steep ledge to the bottom. Furthermore, it was severely eroded along the edges and barely wide enough for the truck. It was, however, dry and sound enough not to crumble away under us. No wonder the park

rangers had said that if we got this far we would be on our own—no vehicle had passed this way in a long time. I shifted into the lowest gear and we went over the rim—down, down, down until we reached the floor.

I noted all the check points and followed the ranger's directions as the track wound about until we came to a very narrow and deep wash, the bottom of which had been cut about two feet deeper by the cloudburst of a few weeks before. There was no way I could get the truck across the gully without a half-day's work with the shovel, and this I was not about to do; we turned around and went back to a fork in the road, where I took the alternate route. Within a mile, the road ended, and because there was no other place to go, I parked and leveled the truck to stay there for as long as we wanted.

We were both anxious to get started the following day: I would look for miniflowers while Katharine photographed the cathedrals in the ever-changing angles of light. I found some flowers that would probably be open by 10:00 that morning, marked their locations with ribbon-bearing stakes, and began to assemble my gear. By this time a brisk wind had started, which made it impossible for me to photograph the flowers where they were growing; I would have to do it in the camper.

In a tiny white cluster no larger than the head of a match, I selected what seemed to be the best flower, and by noon had finished a roll of film. When I went to get the second flower, another

Buckwheat, *Eriogonum leptocladon,* 2.20 mm

cluster of pale yellow and about the size of the first, I noticed that the wind had increased and was blowing dust, so I tightly closed all the windows and vents.

While I was working on the flower, totally oblivious to what was going on, Katharine appeared at the door with her hair in wild disarray and full of sand, clutching her camera. It was then that I realized we were in a full-fledged sandstorm and that it was uncomfortably hot in the camper. I finished with the flower, but there was still another to photograph and I hastened to get it, fervently hoping that it had not wilted or been buried.

It was still there, its five pale lavender petals bravely defying the elements. Because it was late in the day and the flower would not last much longer, I worked furiously to capture its pristine beauty. The fury of the storm had increased and the whole valley was obliterated by flying sand—sagebrush flew horizontally past the windows.

We decided that we might be able to get out of the sand if we were to go back up on the bench and stay there for the night. At the very least, it could not be worse than it was here. The road—as much of it as we could see through the windborne sand—looked awfully steep, and was. It was much steeper than anything we had encountered, and if, for any reason, the truck stalled on the way up, we could be in real trouble.

At the bottom of the grade, I switched on the auxiliary fuel pump, gave a silent prayer, and started up the road. I had never had to call on the engine for this supreme effort, but it did just fine. It was only a few minutes before we were back on top, where we parked next to a big juniper tree about one hundred feet from the rim. We were out of the sand, but the wind was still blowing a full gale. We watched the sand completely obliterate the whole valley; then a cathedral would appear, only to disappear a few moments later. When the sun was low on the horizon, the storm seemed to be over, the sand settled, and while Katharine tried for a few more pictures in the remaining light, I struggled to light the flame in the refrigerator, which had been out all day.

The wind began to blow again during dinner, and by the time we had finished eating, it was singing in the branches of the juniper. It continued to increase, a steady howl indicating its intensity; the truck started to shudder, which made it impossible to continue to read. The flame in the refrigerator was blown out again, but that was the least of my worries. Katharine climbed into bed but could not get to sleep because four feet above the floor, our sleeping quarters were being whipped about most violently. The truck pitched and heaved so badly that I had trouble standing when I changed my position in hopes of maintaining a balance of weight so we wouldn't be blown over.

The fury of the storm increased; a high-pitched scream came from the branches, and the noise was so great that any conversation was impossible. The wind increased still more! The truck shook, shuddered, and heaved as though it was in its dying throes. I glanced at Katharine, who was desperately hanging onto the bed in sheer terror, her eyes wide, her face drawn. I was hanging onto the table with both hands and with one foot braced against its support. Then came an even greater blast as though the wind was determined to blow us off the face of the earth. As the truck heeled way over, I thought we were going all the way. It hung there, suspended, for a fleeting moment and then settled back. The wind stopped as abruptly as a door slamming shut, and there was not a sound.

In the silence, Katharine lay staring over the side of the bed, while I still sat holding onto the table. Both of us were too drained to move or utter a word as we waited for the wind to return from another direction, but it never came. Its last mighty effort had not been enough to destroy us and it had quit trying. The only things that saved us were the ancient juniper tree and the fact that the wind was not hitting the truck full broadside. After awhile, I got up and stepped outside; not a blade of grass was stirring. Wearily, I climbed into bed and found Katharine still shaking.

The following day dawned as mild and as beautiful as anyone could wish for. I checked the truck and retied some gear, all the while wondering how we were going to get out of this place. I had no

Phlox, *Navarretia mellita*, 4.25 mm

doubt but that the dead aspens we had so carefully dodged when coming down the mountain were now lying across the road and blocking it to all traffic. This left the southern route as an alternative, but I had no idea of what the road would be like until we came to the big sandy wash—there could be deep narrow gullies like the one we had come upon back in the valley. It was most unlikely that we would encounter any downed trees along this route because it was well below the aspen, and junipers are not easily blown down. But if we did come upon one, maybe the truck could pull it out of the way, or I could chop through it with the small hand ax.

After everything had been stowed away and tightly secured, we crossed our fingers and started down the road. It wandered about in the grass among the scattered junipers for a mile or so, then dipped over the rim of the bench and descended to the floor of a big, blind wash. I stopped on the rim and inspected the road through binoculars; it didn't look too steep or rough as it went down, but on the bottom it was bad.

We reached the bottom within a few minutes and found the road worse than anticipated. It went along the left side of the wash a few feet above the bottom and had been so badly damaged by the recent cloudburst that parts of it had virtually disappeared under rock and sand; other parts were washed away leaving the track too narrow for the tires to get a good grip. In places where there was a track, it had been deeply cut, six to twelve inches, by the water.

The situation was grim—very grim. We were in one awful predicament. I hesitated for a moment and shifted down into the lowest gear; we inched our way forward. Within one hundred feet I had to stop, get out the shovel, and tear down the sides of a cut so I could get the truck across it. Then more cuts, some so deep that Katharine had to get out, lie on her stomach, and hold up thumb and forefinger to show me how close to the ground the auxiliary gas tank was as the truck inched ahead. When her fingers showed me that the clearance had diminished to less than an inch, I backed up and again used the shovel. Then we would try again. When the truck tilted perilously while trying to cross sand that had been washed from above, I again had to back up and resort to the shovel. Where the track had been partially washed away, we gathered rocks and made fill, then carefully crept across it praying all the while that it would not slide away under the weight of the truck. The shock to the truck was enormous as it crashed and twisted one way and then the other.

Hour after hour we built the road before us: I shoveled and Katharine carried rocks. We were making progress. We passed what I thought was a small spring under the sand in the bottom of the wash, and about a quarter-mile farther, the wash opened and the road improved. We were very tired

Spurge, *Euphorbia micromera,* 1.17 mm

but elated—we had no more road to make. But almost immediately our elation was shattered—the wash we had been following had abruptly turned to the left and there it was in front of us. We had been working so hard on the road that we had forgotten this formidable obstacle, which I had been warned about.

We stopped and walked to the bank to see what it was that had such a frightful reputation. It didn't look good. The wash was more than forty feet wide and dry. Both banks were very steep and I could not get a good run at it, which caused me no little concern because it is essential to move fast and stop for nothing in soft sand. If we got bogged down in this, we would be there until someone came along, which might be for days.

To make it even worse, each bank had been vertically cut a foot or more by the cloudburst. I worked the cuts down with the shovel and noticed that the crown of the first bank was high but thought that we might be able to get over it. When I had finished and was ready to make the attempt, I put the truck in low gear for power and speed, Katharine lay down on her stomach, and I inched the truck forward. But her fingers showed me that the gas tank would not clear the ground, so I backed up and again worked with the shovel. Then I tried it again and this time we went over the bank, but I had to stop when the truck was standing on its nose with the spare tires deeply dug into the sand in the bottom of the wash.

Tired as I was, I had to have a picture of this because otherwise no one would believe it. I got out my camera and walked about in the wash to find the best angles from which to take the pictures. While I was standing and adjusting the camera, I felt a sudden coolness at my feet. I looked down to see water coming over the tops of my boots. Quicksand! I moved fast and, looking back, saw the footprints filled with water while the surrounding sand looked dry as a bone. As long as I kept moving, there was no sign of water, but if I stopped for only a few seconds, I began sinking into the sand.

Now I was alarmed. This was an entirely different ballgame. After I probed every foot of the bot-

Borage, *Lappula texana,* 1.80 mm

tom with the shovel and found it was solid rock about twelve to sixteen inches below the surface, I calmed down—a little. To get across this, the truck would have to unfailingly deliver its absolute maximum effort. I did not find the bottom where I had first been standing!

I backed the truck up to the top of the bank and sat there for a few moments, badly shaken. I asked Katharine to get inside because I wanted as much weight on the tires as possible so they would sink down to bedrock for traction. We were about ready to take the plunge when I heard an auto horn, and in the rearview mirror, I could see a vehicle behind us. This was not exactly the best time for anyone to honk at me, and with fire in my eyes and mayhem in my heart, I boiled out of the truck and headed for the jeep.

In it were two middle-aged men and their wives, all with happy, carefree smiles on their faces. When they saw my mood, their smiles vanished and they kind of scrunched down in their seats. I don't remember ever having been so furious. They did not say a word except to answer my questions in meek and reassuring voices. They had driven from Caineville, a few miles to the east, and had happily come over the road that had taken us hours to repair.

I had not known that there was a road into the valley from the east, and when I heard this, I was angry with the rangers for not having told me about it. I told the tourists that I would try to cross first and if I got stuck they should try to pull me out; likewise, if they got bogged down I would pull them out. Later, I regretted having scared them so badly.

After returning to the truck, I had to sit there for a couple of minutes to quiet my nerves. I started the engine, shifted into the most powerful gear, and jammed the throttle full open. The engine caught with a thunderous bellow, and we charged down into the wash. The truck had been on its nose and now it really was when it went off the bank. The truck shuddered and hesitated on impact with the quicksand, and the front seemed to drop out of sight. The spare tires, half-buried, were pushing a huge wave of sand and water—the consistency of wet concrete. When the rear wheels, driving hard, sank through the sand to bedrock, I felt and heard the crash of the rear step bumper hitting and scraping the bank. We were on the bottom.

As soon as the rear wheels were on the bedrock, the spare tires in front lifted, but the propane and auxiliary gas tank, both bumpers, and the running gear were all pushing quicksand. The exhaust pipes, under the surface, emitted a muffled thunder and blew sand and water all over the place. We crashed across the wash straight as an arrow, and the spare tire mount hit the oncoming bank in an explosion of dry sand. We were up and out of the wash.

We sat there for a few moments and then remembered the jeep behind us; we got out of the truck to see how it fared in the crossing. As soon as it entered the wash it was in trouble and veered wildly out of control. At one point it was headed directly for the spot where I had first discovered the quicksand. The driver desperately tried to keep it on course while its four wheels frantically clawed for a footing, but it was not heavy enough to sink to the bedrock. After making s-turns and trying to go back and forth in the wash, it finally managed to get onto the bank. They drove away without looking at us.

At that moment, a park service pickup truck drove up and stopped. The rangers at headquarters had not expected us to stay more than one night in the valley, and after the storm, they had started to worry and sent this ranger to look for us. He was relieved and pleased to find us all in one piece and surprised that we had crossed the wash without apparent difficulty. He wanted to know about the road behind us and told us that it was good from here to the highway. He also informed us that the Fremont River was not running as high as it had been and that its bottom was good and solid. Then he told us about the storm. It had been the worst in the memory of anyone in the park. The wind velocity had reached 75 mph, the highest ever recorded. When he asked, I told him that where we had been the wind was brisk at times. (With the wind so great in the canyon, what must it have been on the high bench where there was nothing to protect us but one juniper tree?) I don't think the ranger believed me when I told him about the quicksand, for when we drove away, it looked just like any other wash in the hot desert air—dry sand.

The road was not the best, but after what we had been over, it was a boulevard. I noticed that the man who drove the grader had not been overly zealous in his work—he must have been sightseeing. His blade touched the ground only occasionally, and even then it didn't do much good. It was not long before we reached the Pinto Hills, and I then understood the ranger's warnings; anyone caught on these hills in the rain would slide right off.

These low, gently rounded hills are amazingly colored; their clean horizontal strata are brown, purple-gray, white, beige, and brick-red—each form distinct from the others because bentonite does not erode in the same manner as sandstone. There is no vegetation of any kind growing on these hills. They are not very high and cover only a small area—maybe a square mile or so—but they are vivid and unforgettable. Tired as she was, Katharine had to haul out her camera and take pictures.

Five or six miles farther, we came to the Fremont River, a clear stream about forty or fifty feet wide. It didn't look as formidable as I had expected. The road went straight over the steep bank on the outside curve of the stream into the deepest water. When I probed it with the shovel, I found it to be only about 20 inches in depth, and it became shallower toward the opposite bank. The bottom was sound—I could see the rounded stones and hoped that they would not roll under the tires. The crown of the bank looked as though we might be able to squeeze over it, and again Katharine lay down on her stomach to direct me but it was no go; I resorted to the shovel.

While we were doing all this, there were eight or ten cows across the river all lined up, side by side, watching us and expecting, no doubt, that we would get stuck. They were a good audience—they never took their eyes off us. We dipped over the bank and again the truck stood on its nose with the

Borage, *Lappula redowskii* (5 petal), 3.75 mm, Stickseed

spare tires deep in the water. Again, we heard and felt the crash as the rear bumper step hit the bank, and we crossed the river with no problems. About a half-mile farther, we reached the paved highway and I checked the time and the odometer; it had taken us seven hours and forty-five minutes to travel twenty-seven miles.

Twenty minutes later, we limped into the Capitol Reef campground and parked among the gentle trees in the orchard. I noticed that people looked at us carefully with something bordering disdain. The main hatch on the camper had broken and was askew, the dump valve to the holding tank was cracked and leaking badly, bolts had been sheared off the spare tire mount, and Katharine and I looked as though horses had dragged us three miles through the desert. But our efforts had been richly rewarded, for we had photographs of the elusive miniflowers and we had been witness to the capricious beauty of the desert.

"This sky would not be so spectacular without this earth to change and glow and darken under it."

WALLACE STEGNER

On our twenty-eighth expedition, we planned to explore the Sevier Desert, which is south of the Great Salt Lake Desert, to photograph any miniflowers we could find. We had had enough off-the-road travel, so proposed to undertake this journey in a relatively modest manner. I had looked carefully at the official Utah state road map, and while the area was vast and empty, there were some graveled and graded roads through the Sevier that connected with black-top at both the northern and southern boundaries. The nearest town was Delta, a small farming community south of the Sevier. We were anticipating an

Caltrop, *Tribulus terrestris*, 5.00 mm, Puncture Vine

easy trip with relatively cool weather, since it was late September.

It was late in the afternoon and there were heavy thunderstorms in the west and southeast when we arrived at Rowley Junction and turned off the freeway into a gas station. I topped off the gas and water tanks so we had maximum supplies; fifty gallons of gas and twenty-five gallons of water is not too much to carry in this country—one never knows what may happen. We had enough food for a week. When we were ready to leave, I noticed that the storm in the west was rapidly approaching, and its jagged lightning showed that it was not just a mild rainstorm. As we pulled out of the station, the power went off, leaving four or five cars in line

51

behind us without any way to get gasoline.

The map indicated a BLM campground at Simpson Springs, about sixty miles south of Rowley Junction, and with luck, we could get there before it was full dark, but I didn't think we could outrun the storm. The road was not too bad—it was a narrow strip of old blacktop, full of potholes, and covered with sand that had blown across it. We drove a few miles before entering Skull Valley, an apt name for this harsh country. There were low mountains on either side, barren even of desert junipers, and the only vegetation was sparse, low scrub brush that had been beaten almost to death by sandstorms. The sky was a dirty gray from which a sickly yellow light filtered through the storm clouds. The wind began to gust, and the first drops of rain splattered on the windshield.

The road ran straight into the army's Dugway Proving Grounds, a highly secret place where they don't take kindly to strangers who just drop in. The guard, in his immaculate uniform and with a Colt 45 hanging from his waist, stiffly asked us where we were going. When I told him that we were headed for Simpson Springs but that I could not see the road, he pointed to some faint tracks in the sand and indicated that the road was right there in front of me.

Well, the map didn't show anything like this, and I was a little uncertain about going on because I had resolved to stay only on roads and the tracks

Mustard, *Lepidium perfoliatum*, 1.50 mm, Shield Cross

didn't look like much of a road to me. I questioned the guard about it, and he unbent enough to tell us that Simpson Springs was only a few miles away and that lots of people go there. Being where he was with no buildings in sight except his guard house, I suppose that one car a week is lots of people. We had come this far and the great wall of the storm was not far away, so we decided to continue as planned.

As we drove south at the best speed I could muster, the rain slackened a bit, but the wind began to gust more heavily and I was sure that it had blown out the refrigerator flame. The storm was almost on us and it would be black dark in a few minutes. I wanted to find the place while I could still see something.

We arrived at Simpson Springs, according to a sign, at the same moment the storm arrived, and I did not even bother to look for the campground—it was raining too hard. I stopped in an area marked "visitor parking," which seemed level enough for the refrigerator, if it was still operating. It was not, and the wind was too strong to relight it.

While Katharine was preparing dinner, the storm really hit us. The crash of lightning, sometimes only a few dozen yards from us, the thunder, and the wind all made so much noise that we had to shout to each other. The rain poured down in torrents, and the violence of the wind increased to the point where the rig was being shaken so badly that Katharine had trouble keeping the pots and pans on the stove. It takes more than a zephyr to do this—the truck weighs almost 9,000 pounds. This was one of the most violent storms we had experienced—second only to that in Cathedral Valley. Occasionally, as we tried to keep the plates on the table so we could finish dinner, we saw the lights of a few pickup trucks go by as they headed north, and I was relieved on seeing them because they confirmed that the road south was passable and that there might be a few ranches hidden away in this vast desert.

In the morning it was cold. The storm had left snow everywhere but it was not deep—only about one-half of an inch—and it would soon melt. The furnace brought the temperature in the camper up to a comfortable 65 degrees within a few minutes. When I made coffee, I found that the milk in the refrigerator had frozen even though the flame had been out for more than fourteen hours.

It was a beautiful clear morning. The snow seemed to have diamonds sprinkled over it, and through the windows we saw what had attracted lots of people to Simpson Springs. It was the ruins of the old stone buildings that had once been a remount station on the Pony Express route from St. Joseph to Sacramento almost 120 years ago. As we ate breakfast, we could imagine the muffled thunder of hooves as the rider and his sweat-lathered horse broke into view. Two hustlers stood between the house and the corral trying to control a snorting and plunging fresh horse. One of them glanced at his watch, while the rider, a small youth in his teens, gulped down hot food and coffee. They changed the saddle and the mailbags. Few words were spoken. Then the rider was back on the new horse, which kicked dust and sand as it started. Ears back, tail and mane flying, it ran free across the unmarked desert toward the next station thirty miles away.

In the desert, cold morning air is incredibly clear and shadows are very sharp and black; there is nothing in the air to soften or diffuse the light. We could

Buckwheat, *Eriogonum divaricatum,* 1.64 mm

see the mountains about twenty miles south of us, more mountains forty to fifty miles to the west, and about twenty-five miles of the shallow valley we had come through. Everything was glistening white, with bold strokes and splashes of jet black clearly delineating the cliffs, ravines, and scattered desert junipers. By the time we had finished breakfast, cumulus clouds were forming above the mountains; the towering white cumulus in the cobalt blue sky and the subtle pastel colors of the desert—every shade of brown, gray, tan, purple, yellow, and green—were striking in the extreme.

I had planned to start looking for miniflowers after inspecting the truck, because I felt sure that I could find some after the snow melted—and it was fast disappearing. The cumulus clouds foretold of rain, but it would not come until afternoon. If I could find any flowers, and even if it did rain, I could photograph them in the camper.

Turning my attention to the truck, I noticed when I started it that the gas gauge indicated far less gas than the tank should have contained. I switched to the second tank, and the gauge registered full—the gauge was not the problem. When I looked into the engine compartment, small spurts of gas were coming from the pump. This was a major problem, but I was not too alarmed because the truck was equipped with an auxiliary electric pump, which could supply gas to the engine if the main pump were to completely fail. I forgot all about miniflowers.

We reviewed the map to decide whether to go back to Rowley Junction and then into Salt Lake City, or to continue on the graded road to Delta, which was only about forty-five miles south. We could get to Delta in less than two hours, and with any luck, the pump could be repaired that day; then we could return to the Sevier. We decided to go on to Delta. When we drove onto the road, I noticed that the clouds had spread rapidly and the only blue sky was in the east. It was going to rain hard that afternoon.

Within a few miles, the road started to deteriorate, and I had to reduce our speed to below 25 mph. The mood of the desert changed and became threatening. After we had gone about fifteen miles, the sky was so overcast with roiling, low, dark clouds, that I could not see the position of the sun and, with the road winding about, was not sure of the direction in which we were traveling. We came to a fork in the road where there was a sign, "Pony Express Road," and the fork that seemed to go south was the better of the two. I started down it, but after we had gone about one hundred yards, something told me that I had made the wrong choice. I stopped, walked away from the truck, and took a compass reading. We were not headed south, we were going west! We returned to the fork and took the other road, which was less traveled but firm and graded, and it went in the desired direction: southeast. The gas gauge indicated that fuel had been lost, and I calculated that we had not yet

Spurge, *Euphorbia polycarpa*, 2.80 mm

reached the halfway point.

As we continued down the ever-deteriorating road, the valley narrowed to about two miles and the mountains on either side were enveloped in a heavy, dark gray cloud cover that was only a few hundred feet above the ground. There were no trees and no brush—only very sparse dead grasses on the sand and rock. Everything was a dead gray color. Even the light looked gray. Tracks began to branch off the road in all directions, but there were no signs to tell us where they led. I took another compass reading and found that we were still going in a southeasterly direction; we kept trying to find something on the map that corresponded with the road we were on. Behind us a heavy, black rainstorm had started. We didn't have any idea of where we were, nor did we have enough gas to go back.

The night before, there had been a huge cloudburst in the mountains a mile or so south of us and the rushing water had cut deeply across the road: cuts that were from eight to ten inches deep and two to ten feet across. In some places where the road had been graded a foot or more below the surrounding surface, the flow of the water had been so violent that it virtually destroyed the track, and the shock to the truck was enormous. The road joined another at a right angle, and that which went to the right headed straight into the mountains where the cloudburst had occurred; I was not about to take it. We turned left, and I took another compass reading and found that this road went east, but the only thing of any certainty that I could find on the map was a main highway from forty to sixty miles east of where I thought we were.

The clouds had become almost black and they were much lower than they had been. The deep roll of thunder was ominous. Lightning was striking all over the place, and the light was so dim that nothing could be seen distinctly.

After we had gone a few more miles, the road branched into three and there were no signs to guide us, but this intersection seemed to be on the map. The right fork went into the mountains. The middle fork went straight ahead and intersected the black-top from Delta, which I had been hoping to find, but it was almost entirely covered with water for as far as we could see. That which went to the left was merely a track, a jeep road, that curved eastward along the base of the mountains to the north. If a cloudburst was to occur in these mountains, the track could be completely washed out and we would be trapped. We had no choice. The wall of the great storm had moved closer.

I drove as fast as the road would permit, maybe 15 to 20 mph, in an effort to keep ahead of the storm. The map told me nothing, but the compass showed that we were traveling east. The main gas tank was almost empty—only three or four gallons remained—and I switched to the other tank because I didn't want the engine to stop while we were

Pink, *Polycarpon tetraphyllum,* 3.20 mm

going through water. We were barely keeping ahead of the storm when we came to an intersecting graded road and a sign that read, "Delta 32 miles." Our spirits soared—we seemed to be "out of the woods." I could not see very far down the road because it went over a small rise but it was headed away from the mountains and into the flats beyond. Between the intersection and the rise in the ground, there was water across the road in two places, but this was something that we had contended with all day, and we started down the new road.

The first pond was about eighty feet long and fifteen inches deep, but the mud was much slicker than I had expected it to be, and I had to make a quick shift down to keep the truck moving. After the tires had lost and regained traction a few times, we were on higher ground—it had not been too bad. About one hundred yards ahead of us, there was another pond about twice as long as the first, and when we got into it, I found that not only was it much slicker but it was deeper—about twenty inches in all—and I could hear the exhausts burbling. The situation was becoming serious. The truck slowed a little, but I could not go down into a lower gear because the tires were losing traction. I had to depend upon the power of the engine. When I felt the wheels slipping, I immediately let up on the throttle to regain traction, then jammed it to the floor. The strain on the engine was enormous.

Finally, we were through the second pond and when we topped the low rise in the road we saw the third pond and another rise in the ground. This pond was smaller than the others and not quite so deep, but it was much more slippery. Again, I had to resort to rapid throttle work as traction was lost and regained, and when we came out of it, the truck, like an old horse, decided that it had had enough. Four and a half tons are not easy to control when sliding in mud. It was rapid lock-to-lock steering and gentle throttle work that got us up the slight rise, where I stopped. Katharine was pale as a ghost and in a shaken voice suggested that we turn back. I agreed with her because there was no road ahead, only a vast lake with no opposite shore.

I had less than two feet in which to turn the truck around—a difficult task at best. Now it seemed to be impossible because the thin mud was almost as slippery as grease, but after much backing, filling, and sliding, the impossible was accomplished. The problem now was to return to the other road through the three ponds. Should I put on the chains? I decided not to because there was little time. It would take me almost an hour to put the chains on the wheels, and water from the rapidly approaching storm, which looked as though it had developed into another cloudburst, could soon flow into this area and cover the ground we were on. Anyway, we had come through the ponds without chains and I was sure that we could return in the same tracks. They would be deeper but packed more solidly and

Phlox, *Navarretia* (?), 6.25 mm

the truck could follow them without any help from me. Lightning was striking savagely in the west when I eased the truck down into the water and jammed the throttle to the floor.

The tracks were much deeper than expected but not quite so slippery as before. The spare tires, mounted in front of the radiator, began to push mud and water. Then we were out of the pond and headed for the next one, which I feared the most because it was so much longer and deeper than the others. As we approached the pond, I checked the auxiliary pump and saw that it was still furiously pumping despite having been under water. The storm, now blacker than before, shut out most of the light, and heavy wind gusts rippled the water in the pond ahead. Katharine sat staring grimly at the pond we were about to enter, her fists tightly clenched. I gave a silent prayer and we dove into the water.

The truck sank deeper and deeper and began to push a huge wave of mud and water. The instant I felt the tires slip, I let up on the throttle for a fraction of a second to let them regain their grip, then jammed it to the floor—again and again and again—and we kept moving. When we were part way through the pond, I felt a cold chill when, suddenly, the truck sank deeper and slowed. I made a lightning downshift into second gear and prayed that the traction would hold. It held and we continued to move—just barely. The truck pulled as it had never pulled before, then began to rise out of the water and the tires lost traction. Shifting up into third, I felt the tires catch hold, then lose traction and catch again. Finally, we were on higher ground up and out of the water.

As we approached the final pond, the storm, laced with lightning, was coming up fast, and the first raindrops fell. I noticed that the engine temperature had gone straight up and that the auxiliary pump was still working. As the truck entered the water, I jammed the throttle to the floor. Again traction was lost and regained. About midway through the pond, the bottom suddenly dropped away and the spare tires plunged very deep; a huge wave of water almost engulfed them. Second gear, almost instantly. The traction held, and the front of the truck began to rise before the rear wheels hit the hole, and when they did, the truck hesitated as though it just could not do any more. But, with its last ounce of effort, it kept on moving. When we began to climb out of the mud, the engine began to misfire and lose power. Finally, we were on firm sand and gravel. The scene must have looked like a dinosaur emerging from some primordial swamp.

I drove a few more yards to higher ground and when I slowed, the engine died. When I tried to restart it, nothing happened. It had done far more than it was ever intended to do and I let it rest while I walked around the truck to see its condition. I could see nothing but mud. I could not find the exhaust pipes and feared they had been torn off again. The propane and auxiliary gas tanks, which are mounted under the truck, were formless masses of mud, and the wheel wells were filled with mud down to an inch or so above the tires. The running gear was entirely encased in mud, and about an inch of it was spread evenly over the bumper step, which is twenty-one inches above the ground. The truck was carrying at least a thousand pounds of mud and was riding very heavily on its springs.

There was no time to waste, and on the third try, the engine started, but it wasn't feeling at all well—it barely ran. After carefully nursing it along for a bit, I found that it ran best at half or more throttle, so the trouble was something other than water in the ignition. Because the road was bad and I had to use so much throttle to keep the engine from stalling, I had to drive in third gear and, sometimes, second gear, which increased the fuel consumption even more.

The map was of no help at all, but the compass told me that we were still going in an easterly direction. The storm had let us escape, but the terrain, gray and desolate, still held us tightly in its grip. When we came to a sign, "Highway 27 miles," we both cheered, but 27 miles on this road was a long, long way to go. It was late in the afternoon, the light would not hold much longer, and we continued to charge through mud puddles. Sometime later, the road began to improve and I could drive a little faster. As we topped a small hill, we saw, a mile or so away, the highway and the only car in what had seemed an eternity. The sign at the intersection read, "Delta 34 miles."

It was almost dark when we limped into an RV park. When the owner saw the mud-covered apparition in front of him, he stopped short for a moment and then led us to our place for the night. Katharine and I were on the point of total exhaustion.

In the morning, I had my first opportunity to carefully inspect the rig and what I found was appalling. Most of the mud had fallen away from the running gear but it was still packed in the wheelwells and the bumpers, between the spare tires, and it completely concealed the tanks. Stalactites of mud hung from the fenders. Only the faintest hint of the color of the rig could be seen on the upper rear corners of the camper, almost nine feet above the ground. Even the roof had mud on it, thrown up when we had gone too fast through small puddles. The whole thing was a solid tannish gray mass.

The engine started readily but would not idle, and I had to drive it carefully to a garage. The shop superintendent and his mechanics gathered around and stood there staring—none of them said a word. I told them what I wanted, and the chief mechanic opened the hood and then called for the others to come and take a look. The water in the ponds had flowed over the entire engine and filled about one-

Purslane, *Calandrinia ambigua*, 4.50 mm

third of the air cleaner, and sand and gravel were found in the carburetor. It is a wonder that the engine ran at all. Finally, curiosity got the better of him and he asked where we had been. When I told him, he commented on the fact that not many folks went into that area—for obvious reasons. We had definitely had enough of the Sevier Desert for one year.

Turning our travels east again, we met friends on the outskirts of Moab, and it was over dinner that they told us of seeing flowers at Dead Horse Point, just beyond the northern boundary of Canyonlands National Park. On the prospect of finding miniflowers there, we decided to explore the area the following day.

Dead Horse Point is a very small part of a gigantic mesa that juts out into an immense void of total and tortured desolation. The top of the mesa at Dead Horse Point is covered with red slickrock and shallow red sand in which a few dark green junipers and low, dusty brush grow. This place was named by cowboys who used the narrow spit of land two thousand feet above the Colorado River for rounding up horses. Those left behind died of thirst because the vertical descent was too much for even the most rugged animals.

The mesa extends about twenty-five miles west and includes Grandview Point, which overlooks the confluence of the Colorado and Green rivers. Beyond Grandview, we could see the reddish tan cliffs (which gleam like red gold in the first light of the rising sun) towering above the Green River, then the yellow-tan sand of the San Raphael Desert, and still farther, there were the folds of the San Raphael Swell. One hundred and twenty miles to the southwest, the rounded top of 10,000-foot Navajo Mountain could be seen rising from the desert. In the south, forty miles away, the 11,000-foot Abajo Mountains vied for our attention, and in the east, the 12,000-foot La Sals made twenty-five miles seem like nothing as they tried to punch holes in a cloudless azure sky. In the northeast, the huge and spectacular arches carved by the elements from a long-ago red mesa lay only a few miles away. When we looked out over this panorama of vivid color and geologic wonder, we thought of the times we had been beyond every mountain, every cliff and mesa, and every canyon that we could see.

After searching about, I finally found a miniflower, which looked like bits of frost on the small bush on which it was growing. It was silvery white and about three millimeters in its full diameter. I worked on it for more than three hours, and when I had finished, I was tired and discouraged because I had made mistakes.

While I was working on the flower, Katharine made her survey for the best pictures and decided that the early morning light would be the best. She checked and loaded her camera, selected the lenses she would use, and prepared everything to be ready when the sun first struck the cliffs and worked its way down into the desolation below.

The next morning, I found another miniflower growing on a bush similar to the first, and I was almost certain that it was of the same genus but of a different species. It was white with a wash of dark maroon that extended from deep in its throat to almost the tip of its petals and made it look pink. It was smaller than the first, only about 2.5 millimeters in diameter. By one o'clock, I had taken a roll of pictures, then looked for more of these tiny flowers but could not find any.

That night the electrical system in the camper (separate from that in the truck) failed completely, and, subsequently, I found that one of the rubber

San Raphael Reef, Mt. St. Michel

engine mounts had been torn apart by the efforts of the engine. The legacy of the Sevier. We concluded that it was time to go home—if we could get there.

So, once again, we were back on the road, seeing new places, new flowers, new vistas. Our travels have taken us to some of the most spectacular places on earth, each offering a different kind of gift.

We have traveled in deserts from Oregon to Mexico and have always seen something new, something different. Each has its own characteristics: lavender sands, monuments that gleam like gold, black vegetation on black soil, silver-tipped sage for as far as the eye can see, endless miles of sand and rock.

The traveler usually sees only the less attractive parts of the desert because the highways follow the lowest terrain. The best parts are twenty to fifty miles off on either side of the road, over and beyond that range of desert mountains. It is there that one can see the full beauty and feel the ominous nature of the desert. It is not kind, neither is it hostile. It just is.

ABOUT THE AUTHOR

From his earliest days, Robert I. Gilbreath has preferred deserts to mountains or seas. It was in the desert that he and Katharine met the crossroad that would change their lives so completely: miniflowers. With this discovery, they entered the world of museums, botanists, artists, photographers—people intent upon adding to the knowledge and understanding of the world around us. In 1974, the Smithsonian Institution published and displayed Gilbreath's photographs of miniflowers, which at that time were the first-known. During the next ten years, this photographic collection was displayed in most of the major natural history museums across the country.

Robert I. Gilbreath was born and raised near Monte Vista, Colorado, on a sheep ranch. A graduate of Stanford University (1931), he learned to fly airplanes in the navy and flew for thirty years throughout eleven western states in connection with his chemical company. He sold the last of his business interests in 1971 with the intent of charting a new course, and that is just what happened. The Gilbreaths have been married for fifty-three years and have three children and eight grandchildren. Currently enjoying the quietude of retirement, the couple lives south of San Francisco. He is a member of The Explorers Club in New York.

Robert Gilbreath

Katharine Gilbreath

"What is the purpose of the giant cactus? The purpose of the giant cactus is to provide shade for a titmouse."

EDWARD ABBEY

Whatever is wild, leave it wild."

DAVID BROWER

Sandstorm in Monument Valley